Parliament Hill

Simon Rose

Weigl

Published by Weigl Educational Publishers Limited
6325 10th Street SE
Calgary, Alberta T2H 2Z9

Website: www.weigl.ca

Library and Archives Canada Cataloguing in Publication

Rose, Simon, 1961-
    Parliament Hill / Simon Rose.
(Canadian virtual field trip)
Includes index.
ISBN 978-1-77071-479-3 (bound).--ISBN 978-1-77071-482-3 (pbk.)
    1. Parliament Hill (Ottawa, Ont.)--Juvenile literature.
2. Parliament Buildings (Ottawa, Ont.)--Juvenile literature.
I. Title. II. Series: Canadian virtual field trip series

NA4415.C22O77 2012   j725'.110971384   C2011-908208-X

Printed in the United States of America in North Mankato, Minnesota
1 2 3 4 5 6 7 8 9 0 16 15 14 13 12

072012
WEP250612

Editor: Heather Kissock
Design: Terry Paulhus

Every reasonable effort has been made to trace ownership and to obtain permission to reprint copyright material. The publishers would be pleased to have any errors or omissions brought to their attention so that they may be corrected in subsequent printings.

Weigl acknowledges Getty Images as its primary image supplier for this title.

We acknowledge the financial support of the Government of Canada through the Canada Book Fund for our publishing activities.

Contents

What is Parliament Hill?

Located in the heart of downtown Ottawa, Canada's capital city, Parliament Hill serves as the symbolic heart of the country. It is here that the government of Canada makes important decisions on behalf of the country and its citizens. As a result of its impact on the country, the Hill has become a Canadian icon. Every year, Parliament Hill hosts the national Canada Day festivities. Thousands of people go to the Hill on this day to celebrate being Canadian.

Parliament Hill is made up of three main buildings. The Centre Block is the best known and contains the Peace Tower, one of the country's national symbols. This block is home to the **House of Commons** and the **Senate**, Canada's two key **legislative** bodies. The East and West Blocks serve as office buildings for senators, members of **Parliament**, and their staff.

The grounds that surround the buildings of Parliament Hill feature gardens, lawns, and pathways. These areas host a number of statues and memorials of national historic importance. While the Hill is often a site of bustling activity, people can stroll the grounds to get a sense of the country's past, present, and future.

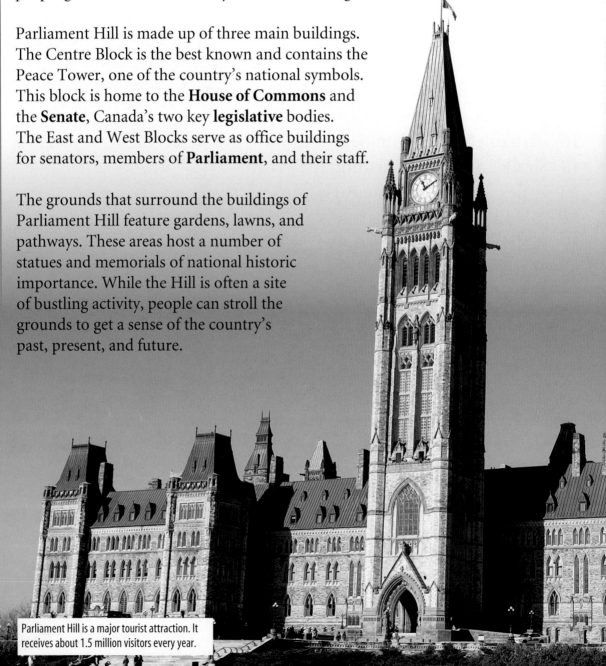

Parliament Hill is a major tourist attraction. It receives about 1.5 million visitors every year.

Snapshot of Ontario

Ontario is located in central Canada. It is the country's most populated province. Ontario shares its eastern border with Quebec and its western border with Manitoba. To the north lies Hudson Bay. To the south are the Great Lakes and the U.S. states of Michigan, Minnesota, New York, Ohio, and Pennsylvania.

INTRODUCING ONTARIO

CAPITAL CITY: Toronto

FLAG:

MOTTO: *Ut incepit Fidelis sic permanet* (Loyal she began, loyal she remains)

POPULATION: 13,372,996 (2011)

JOINED CONFEDERATION: July 1, 1867

CLIMATE: Humid continental in the south with warm summers and cold winters, subarctic in the north

SUMMER TEMPERATURE: Averages between 20° and 30° Celsius

WINTER TEMPERATURE: Averages range from −25°C to −10°C

TIME ZONE: Eastern Standard Time (EST)

MAP LEGEND

- – · – · – International Boundary
- ★ National Capital
- ★ Provincial Capital

0 ——— 200 miles
0 ——— 200 kilometres

Hudson Bay · James Bay · Ontario · Quebec · Thunder Bay · CANADA · Minnesota · Lake Superior · Sault Ste Marie · Sudbury · North Bay · Ottawa · Wisconsin · Lake Huron · Michigan · Kingston · New York · Lake Michigan · Lake Ontario · Toronto · UNITED STATES OF AMERICA · London · Iowa · Lake Erie · Pennsylvania · Illinois · Indiana · Ohio

Ontario Symbols

Ontario has several official symbols. Some symbols represent the features that distinguish the area from other parts of Canada. Others indicate the unique place Ontario has in the history of the country.

COAT OF ARMS

PROVINCIAL MINERAL
Amethyst

PROVINCIAL FLOWER
White Trillium

PROVINCIAL TREE
Eastern White Pine

PROVINCIAL BIRD
Common Loon

A Step Back in Time

Many people were surprised, even shocked, when, in 1858, Ottawa was chosen to be Canada's capital city. It seemed an unlikely candidate. At the time, Ottawa was a small city that sat on the outskirts of civilization. Many people felt that there were other, more suitable, locations, including Toronto, Montreal, and Quebec City. Still, Ottawa had a few advantages. It was located between the former provinces of Canada East and Canada West, and it was a reasonable distance from the United States border. It seemed a smart choice for a capital city.

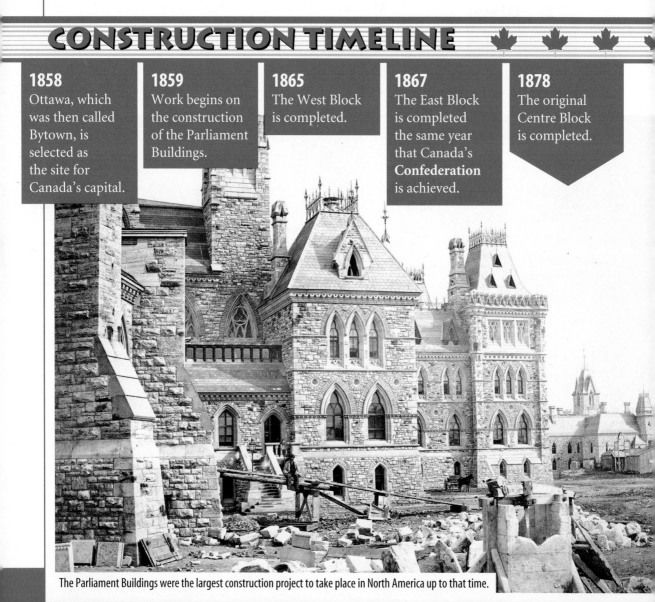

CONSTRUCTION TIMELINE

1858
Ottawa, which was then called Bytown, is selected as the site for Canada's capital.

1859
Work begins on the construction of the Parliament Buildings.

1865
The West Block is completed.

1867
The East Block is completed the same year that Canada's **Confederation** is achieved.

1878
The original Centre Block is completed.

The Parliament Buildings were the largest construction project to take place in North America up to that time.

Once the decision was made on the capital city, the search for the site of the new Parliament Buildings began. At the top of the list was an open area on a limestone cliff above the Ottawa River. The land sat in the middle of town, but at a height that would allow the buildings to be seen for kilometres. It was deemed the most appropriate setting for Canada's Parliament Buildings.

The escarpment on which Parliament Hill sits once served as a landmark for Aboriginal peoples and European explorers travelling on the river.

1910
Another **wing** is added to the East Block.

1916
Fire destroys the Centre Block on February 3.

1922
The rebuilding of the Centre Block is completed.

1927
The Peace Tower is completed and dedicated to those Canadians who died in World War I.

1976
Parliament Hill and the Parliament Buildings are designated as a **National Historic Site**.

Caused by a carelessly discarded cigar, the fire of 1916 left most of the Centre Block ruined.

The Peace Tower was built as part of the reconstruction after the fire. It is considered to be one of Canada's most identifiable landmarks.

Parliament Hill's Location

Parliament Hill is situated on the south shore of the Ottawa River. The cliff on which it stands was considered a landmark for hundreds of years, both to the Aboriginal Peoples of the area and to the early European traders and settlers. During the building of the Rideau Canal, which opened in 1832, the area was occupied by the military. The plan was for the military to build a large fort on the hill. However, once Ottawa was chosen as the site of Canada's capital, planners decided to build the country's Parliament Buildings on the hill instead.

Prior to the construction of the Parliament Buildings, Parliament Hill was known as Barrack Hill. Barracks are buildings that house soldiers.

Parliament Hill Today

Parliament Hill is one of Canada's most recognizable landmarks and a major tourist attraction. Visitors from all over the world come to tour the buildings and grounds. Here, they learn about the basic principles of **democracy** and **representative government** under which the country is governed.

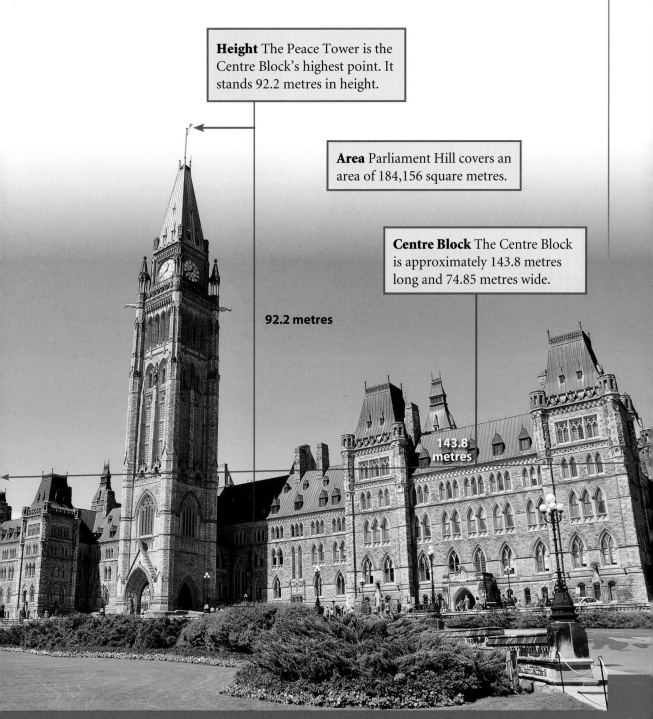

Height The Peace Tower is the Centre Block's highest point. It stands 92.2 metres in height.

Area Parliament Hill covers an area of 184,156 square metres.

Centre Block The Centre Block is approximately 143.8 metres long and 74.85 metres wide.

92.2 metres

143.8 metres

Key Structures on Parliament Hill

Most of the structures on Parliament Hill are situated around a large quadrangle lawn. The lawn serves as a connecting point for the buildings, statues, and memorials found on the Hill.

Queen's Gates The south front of Parliament Hill is marked by the wrought iron fence known as the Wellington Wall. At the centre of the wall are the Queen's Gates. These act as the formal entrance to Parliament Hill. The Queen's Gates were built in 1872. They open onto Ottawa's Wellington Street.

The Wellington Wall and the Queen's Gates were restored to their original condition in 1992 at a cost of $5 million.

The shield for Nunavut is not on the fountain's ledge. This is because Nunavut did not become a territory until 1999.

Centennial Flame Beyond the Queen's Gates is the Centennial Flame. The flame was first lit on New Year's Day 1967 by then Prime Minister Lester B. Pearson to commemorate Canada's first 100 years as a country. The flame forms the central part of a fountain. The ledge around the fountain is surrounded by the shields of the country's territories and provinces. The flame and fountain signify Canada's unity.

West Block The West Block contains meeting and office space, which is used mainly by members of Parliament and their staff. The building houses the Confederation Room, a grand **reception room** that features six crystal chandeliers and a mirrored wall. The West Block is not open to the public.

The West Block has grown since it was first built. A new wing and tower were added in 1878. Another tower was built onto the building in 1906.

A statue of Thomas D'Arcy McGee, one of Canada's Fathers of Confederation, stands outside the Centre Block.

Statues In 1885, a statue of Sir George-Étienne Cartier, one of the **Fathers of Confederation**, was unveiled on Parliament Hill. This was the first statue on the site. Since then, other statues have been erected. Parliament Hill now includes statues of Sir John A. Macdonald and Wilfrid Laurier, Canada's first francophone prime minister, as well as Queen Victoria and Queen Elizabeth II.

East Block Like the West Block, the East Block is mainly an office building. Many senators have their offices in this building. Several of the East Block's rooms have been recreated to give visitors a sense of Canada's early political scene. The restored offices of Sir John A. Macdonald, Canada's first prime minister, are found in the East Block.

The East Block was built in two stages. The main part of the building was constructed along with the other Parliament Buildings. In 1910, a wing was added to the back of the building.

Centre Block The Peace Tower is the Centre Block's most dominant feature. Its height indicates the importance of the building to the Canadian government. It is here that the House of Commons and the Senate are located. These two government bodies make key decisions for the country.

The clock in the Peace Tower is accompanied by a carillon, made up of 53 bells. These are rung at noon on weekdays as well as for recitals and special events.

VIRTUAL TOUR

At 10:00 a.m. every morning through the summer months, visitors can watch the Changing of the Guard ceremony. Soldiers march and bands play as a new shift takes over the job of guarding the Parliament Buildings.

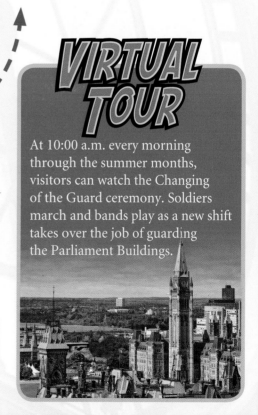

Inside the Centre Block

Canada's Parliament consists of the House of Commons and the Senate. Both are located in the Centre Block of Parliament Hill. While the Centre Block was built to house the government, it also features rooms and halls that pay tribute to Canada and its history.

Confederation Hall The main entrance to the Centre Block leads directly into Confederation Hall. The hall serves as the central core of the building and provides access to all other parts of the Centre Block. A huge column stands in the middle of the circular hall. It is surrounded by several arches and pillars.

The design of Confederation Hall has been influenced by buildings found in England.

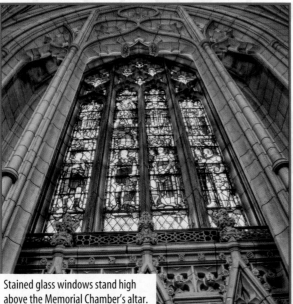

Stained glass windows stand high above the Memorial Chamber's altar.

Memorial Chamber
The Memorial Chamber, which is only 7.3 metres by 7.3 metres, is located on the third floor of the Peace Tower. The **focal point** of the room is the Altar of Remembrance, which pays tribute to those Canadians who died in the service of their country. The names of these men and women are listed in the seven Books of Remembrance that are distributed throughout the room.

Library of Parliament The Library of Parliament is located at the rear of the Centre Block. It is separated from the rest of the building by a corridor. The library houses a variety of research resources for people who work in Parliament. The main reading room has a **vaulted** ceiling and a white marble statue of the young Queen Victoria.

The Library of Parliament is the only part of the original Centre Block to survive the 1916 fire intact.

The Senate is the upper house of Canada's Parliament. It reviews all laws drafted in the House of Commons.

Senate The Senate chamber, located at the east end of the Centre Block, is more richly decorated than the House of Commons. The Chamber has a throne for the Queen or the Governor General and large paintings on the walls. **Heraldic symbols** and gold leaf decorate the ceiling and two huge bronze chandeliers, each weighing 1.8 tonnes, hang from it. The Senate chamber is often called the Red Room because of its red carpets, drapes, and upholstery.

House of Commons Canada's system of government is based on that of Great Britain. As a result, the chamber of the House of Commons is similar to its counterpart in London. The prime minister and members of his or her party sit on one side of the House. The **opposition** parties sit on the other side. The speaker sits between the two sides at the north end of the House. It is the speaker's job to keep order in the House. A section called the Upper Gallery runs around the second level of the room. The public can sit here to observe the speeches and debates taking place in the House.

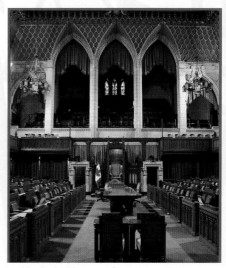

Unlike the British House of Commons, which uses benches, the Canadian chamber has individual chairs and tables for its members of Parliament.

Big Ideas Behind Parliament Hill

When planning the buildings and grounds of Parliament Hill, the planners wanted the area to appear stately, formal, and suited to its purpose. The design of the buildings and the materials to be used were of the utmost importance.

The Peace Tower alone has about 370 original carvings, including several gargoyles and grotesques.

Neo-Gothic Style

The buildings on Parliament Hill have been designed in the neo-Gothic style, a style quite popular in the late 1800s. Neo-Gothic structures draw their inspiration from **medieval** times. They are known for their steep roofs and thick stone walls as well as their stone carvings of **gargoyles** and **grotesques**. Neo-Gothic **architecture** is associated with parliamentary democracy, which is reflected in the design of the British Parliament Buildings in London. The style was chosen for the Canadian Parliament Buildings to emphasize the country's loyalty to Great Britain.

The Properties of Stone

Natural materials, such as stone, have always been used for building. This is because stone is long-lasting and able to withstand fire and freezing. The buildings on Parliament Hill are made from 24 types of stone. The external walls are made mostly of Nepean sandstone, and the inside walls are made mainly of Tyndall stone, a type of limestone. Both sandstone and limestone are considered soft stones. This means they are easy to shape and carve. This helped the building designers create the sculptures and carvings of the neo-Gothic style.

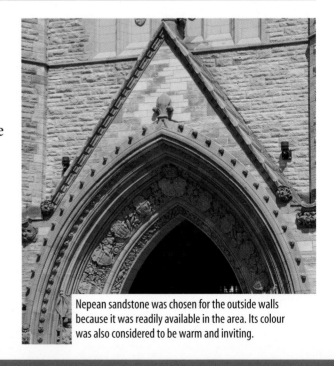

Nepean sandstone was chosen for the outside walls because it was readily available in the area. Its colour was also considered to be warm and inviting.

Science at Work at Parliament Hill

Building any structure requires planning, physical labour, and technology. The people who worked on the Parliament Buildings were part of a careful, painstaking process.

The positioning of the Parliament Buildings' stonework is critical in helping the structures support their own weight.

Withstanding Weight

Load is an important concept in the planning of any building. Load is the weight of pressure carried by an object. The Parliament Buildings were constructed on a solid limestone cliff. The limestone was more than capable of supporting the weight of the buildings. Stone masons then had to make sure that the buildings were constructed to support their own weight and the weight of their contents. They placed the stones in rows on top of each other. This sent their weight directly down into the buildings' **foundation**. The foundation and the limestone underneath then took the brunt of the load.

Transporting Sandstone

The sandstone used to build the outer walls of the Parliament Buildings came from the nearby town of Nepean. Trucks had not been invented yet, so the rock had to be brought to the site by horse-drawn wagons. Wagons use wheels and axles to move across the ground. The wheel and axle is a two-part simple machine. Wheels rotate, so they reduce **friction** between the moving object and the ground. The axle is the structure that attaches the wheel to the rest of the wagon. By using wagons with wheels and axles, builders could move large loads of sandstone.

Wheels on a wagon only touch the ground at one spot at a time. This keeps the rest of the wagon off the ground, resulting in less friction.

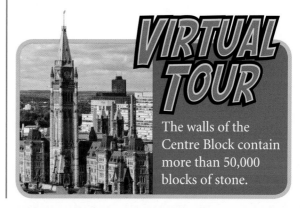

VIRTUAL TOUR

The walls of the Centre Block contain more than 50,000 blocks of stone.

Parliament Hill's Builders

When it was decided to construct Canada's Parliament Buildings in Ottawa, the government asked for designs to be submitted. They received 298 drawings for the proposed buildings. Shortly after a design was chosen in August 1859, workers began the job of building Parliament Hill.

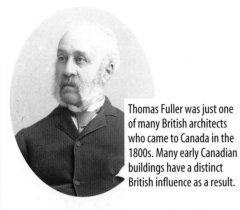

Thomas Fuller was just one of many British architects who came to Canada in the 1800s. Many early Canadian buildings have a distinct British influence as a result.

Thomas Fuller and Chilion Jones Architects, Centre Block

The building of the Centre Block was awarded to Thomas Fuller and Chilion Jones. While Chilion Jones had been born in Canada in 1838, Thomas Fuller was born in Great Britain. He had immigrated to Canada after living in the Caribbean island of Antigua for a short time. The two men met shortly after Fuller arrived in Canada and soon formed a business partnership. Their first major project was to design St. Stephen-in-the-Fields Church in Toronto. When their company was awarded the job of constructing the Centre Block, Fuller took on the role of chief architect and worked closely with architect Charles Baillairge to make the building a reality.

Thomas Stent and Augustus Laver
Architects, East and West Blocks

Augustus Laver worked under architects in England before becoming an architect himself.

Thomas Stent and Augustus Laver were given the job of designing the East and West Blocks. August Laver received his architectural training in Great Britain. After living the United States for a short time, he eventually moved to Ottawa, where he formed a partnership with another architect, Thomas Stent. Stent was also British and had moved to Canada in 1858. Together, the two men began developing designs for buildings in the Ottawa area. After being awarded the job of building the East and West Blocks, however, they were both dismissed from the job when the cost of construction exceeded the budget for the project. Their partnership dissolved shortly after.

Laver and Stent were the second choice, behind Fuller and Jones, to design the Centre Block. This may explain why the design of East and West Blocks complements that of the Centre Block so well.

Quarry Workers

Much of the sandstone used in the buildings on Parliament Hill came from a **quarry** in nearby Nepean, Ontario. Cutting rock from a quarry is hard, dirty, and dangerous work. Quarry workers used explosives and hand tools, such as **chisels** and hammers, to cut the rock into large slabs. The heavy rock was then loaded, using pulleys, onto horse-drawn carts and delivered to construction crews on Parliament Hill. Today, quarry workers use drilling machines and explosives to break up rock.

Today's quarry workers have the benefit of working with power tools. Workers in the 1800s had to rely on basic tools such as chisels and hammers to cut rock.

Masons

Stonemasons played an important role in the construction of the buildings on Parliament Hill. A stonemason is a professional who works with stones or bricks. When raw slabs of sandstone arrived at the construction site, each piece had to be shaped and smoothed. Masons used an L-shaped tool called a square to measure the pieces. Each block had to be a specific size so that it fit in place properly. The masons would scratch the measurements onto the rock. Then, with a chisel and a mallet, they would chip away at it until it was the correct size and shape.

Masons have to know how to cut and place stonework so that the structure it is part of remains sturdy over time.

Labourers

Labourers play a key role at any construction site. They get the materials into the hands of the people who need them. They do this by carrying the materials on their shoulders, carting them in wheelbarrows, and loading them onto trucks and carts. Labourers help keep job sites clean. They know how to use tools, such as saws and hammers, and can operate a variety of construction equipment. During the construction of the Parliament buildings, labourers were responsible for much of the everyday building. They carried supplies to and around the site and helped with the construction process itself.

Labourers can do a range of work, making them indispensable on a construction site.

Similar Structures Around the World

The neo-Gothic movement first appeared in the late 1700s. By the end of the 19th century, however, buildings in this style were being built in various parts of the world. Many of these structures remain standing today, a testament to the construction methods of their builders.

Palace of Westminster

BUILT: 1840 to 1870
LOCATION: London, England
DESIGN: Charles Barry
DESCRIPTION: The British Houses of Parliament were destroyed in a fire in 1834. The present building, known as the Palace of Westminster, was completed in 1870. The Palace has 1,000 rooms, 3.2 kilometres of corridors, and 100 staircases. The building has three main towers. The most famous of these towers is the 97.5-metre high clock tower, containing the bell known as Big Ben.

The University of Glasgow was founded in 1451. It moved to its current location in 1870.

University of Glasgow

BUILT: 1870
LOCATION: Glasgow, Scotland
DESIGN: George Gilbert Scott
DESCRIPTION: The main building of the University of Glasgow towers high into the city's skyline. Completed in 1870, the neo-Gothic building features a tall central tower and accompanying spire.

The Palace of Westminster is one of Great Britain's most enduring symbols.

New Town Hall

BUILT: 1867 to 1908
LOCATION: Munich, Germany
DESIGN: Georg von Hauberrisser
DESCRIPTION: The New Town Hall is the home of Munich's city government, including the mayor's office and various administrative departments. The building faces onto a large square known as the Marienplatz. The main tower features the Rathaus Glockenspiel, in which mechanical figures reenact stories from the 16th century three times a day.

The New Town Hall in Munich has 400 rooms.

Ormond College is the largest residential college at the University of Melbourne. It serves as home to almost 400 teachers and students.

Ormond College

BUILT: 1879
LOCATION: Melbourne, Australia
DESIGN: Joseph Reed
DESCRIPTION: Ormond College is part of the University of Melbourne. The foundation stone was laid in November 1879, and the college was formally opened in March 1881. Like most neo-Gothic buildings, the college's main building features a central tower. This tower was based on the one at the University of Glasgow. The tower at Ormond College stands 50.3 metres tall.

Issues Facing Parliament Hill

A massive $1 billion restoration program has been taking place in the Parliament Buildings since 2002 and is expected to continue until at least 2020. Some of the repairs are needed due to the age of the buildings, but some structural damage has been caused by environmental factors.

WHAT IS THE ISSUE?

Some of the Parliament Buildings are more than 100 years old. Their exteriors have deteriorated over time.	The interiors of the Parliament Buildings are very old and in need of upgrading.	Ottawa's winter climate involves a freeze-thaw cycle, which damages masonry over time.

EFFECTS

Cracks appeared in masonry walls, and the **mortar** holding the stones together was damaged. The Centre Block's copper roof had become **corroded** and was leaking.	Mechanical and electrical systems date from long ago. Many of the walls of older buildings were insulated with **asbestos**, which is now known to be a serious health risk.	Rain seeping through cracked stone, plus moisture from freezing and thawing in winter, has weakened the masonry. If left unchecked, the buildings could eventually collapse.

ACTION TAKEN

Restoration work involved dismantling damaged stonework and rebuilding it. The copper roof and windows were also replaced.	Restoration work has involved the removal of asbestos, renovations of the interiors, and the upgrading of electrical, mechanical, plumbing, and emergency systems.	Although this affects all of the buildings, parts of the West Block have been covered with high fencing to protect people from falling stone until the building can be restored.

A House of Cards

When planning a building, architects have to decide what techniques will be used to ensure that the structure will support its load and not fall apart. They have to consider not only the materials to be used, but how those materials will be positioned to make a strong and durable structure.

This activity will demonstrate how the arrangement of materials is a key factor to making a strong building.

Materials
a deck of playing cards

Instructions
1. Take two cards from the deck. Place them so that the tops rest against each other and the bottoms are about 5 centimetres apart. They should form an upside-down "V".

2. Take two more cards and repeat Step 1, positioning these cards about 1 centimetre away from the other two.

3. Place another card horizontally over the tops of the two sets of cards.

4. Build another upside-down "V" on top of the horizontal card.

5. Add more sets to the bottom row of cards. Continue to cover this row with horizontal cards, and build upwards.

6. Keep building the structure outwards and upwards.

How many levels were you able to build before the house fell? What do you think caused the house of cards to fall? What would you do differently next time to build a stronger structure?

Parliament Hill Quiz

Q What is the name of the architectural style used to design the Parliament Buildings?

A Neo-Gothic

Q Who was depicted in the first statue built on Parliament Hill?

A Sir George-Étienne Cartier

Q What type of stone was used for the construction of the outside walls of the Parliament Buildings?

A Nepean sandstone

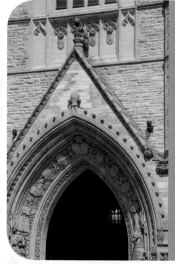

Q How tall is the Peace Tower?

A 92.2 metres

Further Research

You can find more information about Parliament Hill, its features, and its history at your local library or on the internet.

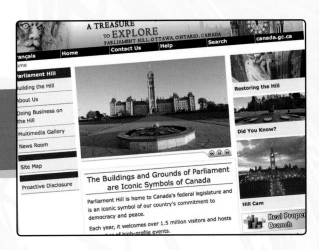

Learn more about the history behind Parliament Hill at **www.parliamenthill.gc.ca**

For more information about visiting Parliament Hill, go to **www.parl.gc.ca/visitors**

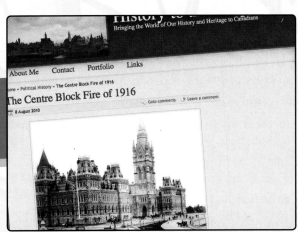

Find out more about the Centre Block fire of 1916 at **http://historytothepeople.ca/2010/08/ the-centre-block-fire-of-1916/**

Glossary

architecture: the design of buildings and other structures

asbestos: a mineral that is resistant to heat, flames, and chemical action

chisels: metal tools with a sharpened edge at one end that is used to chip, carve, or cut stone

Confederation: the union of three British colonies that formed Canada

corroded: eaten or worn away by a chemical action

democracy: a form of government in which the supreme power is held by the people

Fathers of Confederation: the political leaders who attended the meetings that led to Canada's Confederation

focal point: a place that the eye is naturally drawn to

foundation: a construction below the ground that distributes the load of a building or other structure

friction: a force that slows down motion when surfaces slide against each other

gargoyles: stone carvings in the shape of a human or animal that decorate a building and act as spouts

grotesques: carvings of fantastical creatures

heraldic symbols: the official symbols of a family, state, etc.

House of Commons: the main lawmaking body of Parliament

legislative: law-making

medieval: relating to the Middle Ages, between the years 476 to 1453 AD

mortar: a bonding material used in masonry

National Historic Site: a place that has been designated as important to the history of Canada

opposition: the political parties that are not in power

Parliament: the government of Canada, made up of the House of Commons and the Senate

quarry: an open pit from which stone is obtained

reception room: a room set aside to greet people

representative government: a system of government in which elected individuals represent the people

Senate: one of the lawmaking bodies of the Canadian parliament

vaulted: arched

wing: a structure attached to the side of a building

Index